ANTONIN

QUINTET

for 2 Violins, Viola, Violoncello
and Double-bass (Kontrabaß)
G major/G-Dur/Sol majeur
Op. 77

Ernst Eulenburg Ltd

London · Mainz · Madrid · New York · Paris · Prague · Tokyo · Toronto · Zürich

Quintet

I

Antonin Dvořák, op. 77
1841 - 1904

Ernst Eulenburg Ltd

A

4

E.E. 6059

8

E grandioso

12

H

L

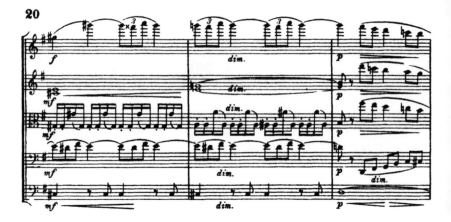

24

SCHERZO

II

Allegro vivace (M.M. ♩= 88)

E.E. 6059

28

32

TRIO

L'istesso tempo, quasi allegretto

34

E

Da Capo Scherzo al Fine

III

Poco andante (M.M. ♩ = 69)

E.E. 6059

40

C

ritard. a tempo

rit. a tempo

IV

FINALE
Allegro assai (M.M. ♩ =132)

50

58

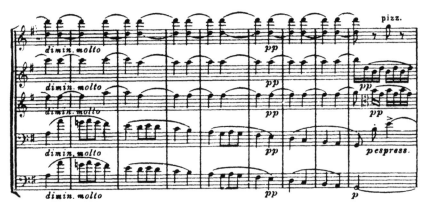

E.E. 6059

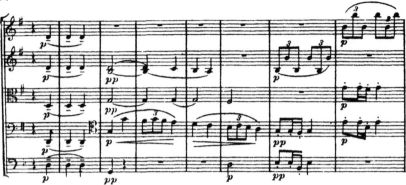

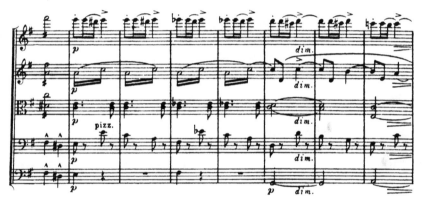

68

E.E. 6059